Best of Graphis
Photo II

PAGE ONE PUBLISHING

In the case of some of the reproductions in this book it proved impossible to locate the originals, despite careful research. They were, however, considered to be of such importance that the decision was taken by the present publisher to reproduce from other published sources.

Cover Photographer: Matthew Rolston

© 1993 by Graphis Press Corp., Dufourstrasse 107, CH-8008 Zürich, Switzerland

© 1993 for this edition by Page One Publishing Pte Ltd, Singapore
Distributed worldwide by Könemann Verlagsgesellschaft mbH, Bonner Str. 126, D-50968 Köln

Designed by Peter Feierabend, Berlin
Text: Ansgar Pächter, Cologne
English translation: Michael Hulse, Cologne
French translation: Michèle Schreyer, Cologne

Printed in Singapore
ISBN 981-00-4769-X

Foreword

This volume contains a variety of advertising and fashion photographs as well as documentary, landscape, animal and portrait photos. If you leaf through slowly but without pausing over individual pictures you will see that the layout was conceived in such a way as to structure two-page selections. The two to seven photographs that appear on any two-page spread go together well in terms of form and content. What is it that creates our sense of visual inter-connection and harmony? And what is its implication for the individual photo? In trying to answer these questions, let us concentrate on the content of the shots.

One straightforward kind of combination is to put two animal photographs together – say, a puma and a rhinoceros (pp. 60/61). Our initial feeling that the pictures go well together is reinforced by the fact that one is a frontal view, one a rear. Arguably we refrain from examining the photos more closely because the similarity (two animals) and the difference (front/rear) are so readily grasped. We have a rapid sense of having exhausted the "meaning" of the photographs.

If a human face had been reproduced on the page opposite the puma's, our attention to the animal's expression and gaze would probably have been greater. At least, our sense of similarity and difference would have been steered in a different direction. (What lies behind an animal's gaze, and what behind a human being's? This or something like it would have been what we wondered.) This is a simple example of the way perception depends on context.

Another example is the photographs on pp. 50/51. The six portraits by Russian photographer Sergei Leontiev, and the picture of a triumphal arch sinking into the landscape by his fellow countryman Valery Potapov, were not originally taken to be seen in relation to each other. In very different ways they seem to convey Russian realities in the Gorbachev era. The portraits show people "as they are" rather than posing them to advantage. Reality is not hidden behind the façade of ideological commonplaces (the state, the Party, the workers), displaced by wishful thinking, or otherwise prettified, and thus the photographs claim to be considered truthful. The contrast is between people as individuals on the one side, and the triumphal arch, symbol of state or at least anti-individual power, sinking into the desolate country on the other, proclaiming the fall of the old system and its historical pretension.

This interpretation arguably goes too far. At all events, it depends on a sense that these photographs are complementary in statement. To think what remarkable effects can be achieved by juxtaposition after the event!

This book contains various juxtapositions that will guide the eye and prompt thought. Anyone, in other words, can carry on where the present foreword leaves off.

Vorwort

Dieser Band enthält Werbe- und Modephotographien sowie Dokumentar-, Landschafts-, Tier- und Porträtphotographien in bunter Folge. Wer die Seiten des Bandes langsam, ohne längeres Verweilen bei einzelnen Photographien durchblättert, wird aber bemerken, daß das Layout einer Ästhetik der komponierten Doppelseite folgt: Die zwei bis sieben Photographien einer Doppelseite passen inhaltlich und formal gut zusammen. Wodurch wird diese Harmonie der Bildzusammenhänge erzeugt? Und was bewirkt sie für das einzelne Photo? Konzentrieren wir uns bei der Beantwortung dieser Fragen auf die Bildinhalte.

Ein einfacher Kombinationstyp ist die Zusammenstellung zweier Tierphotos, eines Pumas und eines Rhinozerosses (S. 60/61). Der vordergründige Eindruck des Zusammenpassens der Photographien wird durch zwei konträre Ansichten – hier ist es das Gesicht, dort das Hinterteil des Tieres – noch gesteigert. Vermutlich wird das Weiterlesen des einzelnen Photos dadurch verkürzt, daß man jene Ähnlichkeit (Tier / Tier) und diese Differenz (vorne / hinten) so schnell konstatiert. Der „Sinn" der Photos ist für den Betrachter damit fast schon erschöpft.

Hätte man dem „Gesicht" des Pumas auf der einen Seite das Gesicht eines Menschen auf der anderen Seite gegenübergestellt, würde die Aufmerksamkeit des Betrachters auf den Blick und den Gesichtsausdruck des Pumas dadurch wahrscheinlich gesteigert. Dem Wahrnehmungsschema der Ähnlichkeits- und Differenzfeststellung jedenfalls wäre eine andere Richtung vorgegeben. (Was verbirgt sich hinter dem Blick des Tieres und was hinter dem eines Menschen? Diese oder eine ähnliche Frage hätte sich dem Betrachter vielleicht gestellt.) Wir haben hier ein einfaches Beispiel für die Kontextabhängigkeit der Wahrnehmung.

Ein anderes Beispiel finden wir in der Zusammenstellung der Photographien auf der Doppelseite 50/51. Die sechs Porträtphotographien des russischen Photographen Sergej Leontiev und das Photo eines in einer Landschaft versinkenden Triumphbogens seines Landsmannes Valery Potapov stehen in keinem ursprünglich intendierten Zusammenhang. Auf sehr unterschiedliche Weise scheinen sie die russische Wirklichkeit der Gorbatschow-Ära zu reflektieren. Die Porträtphotographien zeigen Individuen „so, wie sie sind", also nicht vorteilhaft in Szene gesetzt. Indem sie die Wirklichkeit nicht hinter der Fassade eines ideologischen Allgemeinen – der Staat, die Partei, die Werktätigen – verbergen, durch Wunschbilder ersetzen oder in irgendeiner anderen Weise beschönigen, demonstrieren die Photographien ihren Anspruch auf Aufrichtigkeit. – Während auf der einen Seite die Menschen als Individuen zum Vorschein kommen, versinkt auf der anderen ein mächtiger Triumphbogen, Symbol staatlicher, jedenfalls überindividueller Macht im Boden einer öden Landschaft und kündet vom Untergang des alten Systems und seinen historischen Anmaßungen.

Vielleicht ist diese Interpretation zu gewagt. Richtig ist, daß sie zum Teil darauf beruht, daß sich die Photographien ergänzen und in ihren Aussagen gegenseitig zu stützen scheinen. Bemerkenswert, was ihre nachträgliche Zusammenstellung bewirkt!

Es gibt in diesem Band noch einige andere Zusammenstellungen von Photographien, die den Blick des Betrachters lenken. Er kann also diesen Text aus seiner Sicht fortsetzen, wenn er mag.

Préface

Cet album contient une série multicolore de photographies publicitaires, de photos de mode ainsi que de photos documentaires, de paysages, d'animaux et de portraits. Mais celui qui feuillette ces pages lentement, sans s'attarder sur les photographies, remarque que la composition suit une logique de l'esthétique à l'intérieur de la page double: les deux à sept photographies que contient une page double correspondent entre elles au niveau de la forme et du contenu. Comment atteindre cette harmonie des images? Et qu'apporte-t-elle à la photo isolée? Pour répondre à ces questions nous concentrons notre attention sur le contenu des images.

Un type de combinaison simple est la réunion de deux photos d'animaux, un puma et un rhinocéros (p. 60/61). La première impression de correspondance est encore rehaussée par deux vues contraires – ici le visage, là l'arrière-train de l'animal. La lecture des photos qui suivent sera probablement raccourcie par le fait qu'on constate aussi vite les ressemblances (animal/animal) et les différences (devant/derrière). La signification des photos est alors déjà presque épuisée pour le spectateur.

Si on avait placé le «visage» du puma sur une page et le visage d'un homme sur la page ci-contre, l'observateur aurait vraisemblablement accordé plus d'attention au regard et à l'expression du puma. Le schéma de perception constatant la ressemblance et la différence aurait en tout cas pris une autre direction. (Que cache le regard de l'animal et que cache celui de l'homme? Le spectateur se serait peut-être posé cette question ou une autre semblable). Nous avons ici un exemple simple de la manière dont la perception dépend du contexte.

Un autre exemple de photos placées sur une double page: (p. 50/51) les six portraits du photographe russe Sergej Leontiev et la photo d'un arc de triomphe sombrant dans le paysage de son compatriote Valery Potapov n'ont au départ pas de rapport intentionnel. De manière très différente ils semblent refléter la réalité russe de l'ère Gorbatcheff. Les portraits montrent des individus «tels qu'ils sont», c'est-à-dire sans mise en scène avantageuse. Du fait qu'ils ne cachent pas la réalité derrière la façade d'une généra-lité idéologique – l'Etat, le Parti, les Travailleurs, qu'ils ne l'idéalisent pas ou qu'ils ne l'embellissent pas d'une manière ou d'une autre, les photographes démontrent leur droit à la sincérité. Alors que sur une page les gens apparaissent comme des individus, l'autre page nous montre un arc de triomphe qui s'enfonce – symbole d'une puissance nationalisée ou du moins supra-individuelle – dans le sol d'un paysage désertique et annonce le déclin de l'ancien système et ses prétentions historiques.

Peut-être cette interprétation est-elle trop osée. Il est vrai qu'elle repose en partie sur le fait que les photographies se complètent et semblent se soutenir mutuellement dans ce qu'elles veulent exprimer. L'effet de cette disposition a posteriori est remarquable.

On trouvera dans cet album d'autres agencements de photographies qui guident le regard du spectateur. S'il le désire, rien ne l'empêche de poursuivre ce texte comme il l'entend.

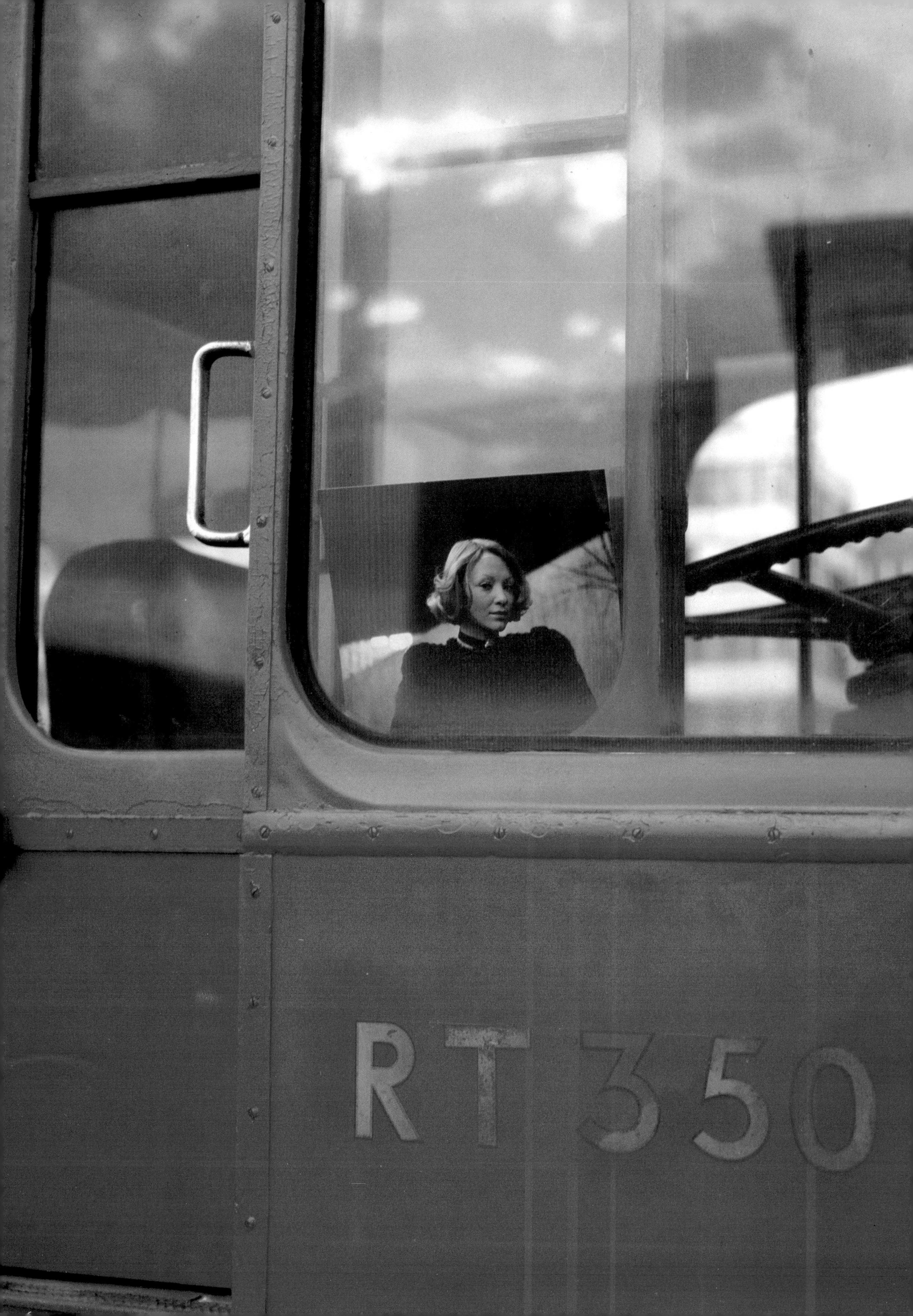
RT 350

Christian von Alvensleben
Fashion shot

Thomas Lüttge
The image in the image

Eberhard Grames
Winter on Hokkaido

Klaus D. Francke
Iceland

Michael Dannemann
Photographic portrait

Richard Fischer
The Great Piers

Ross Feltus
Children's fashion

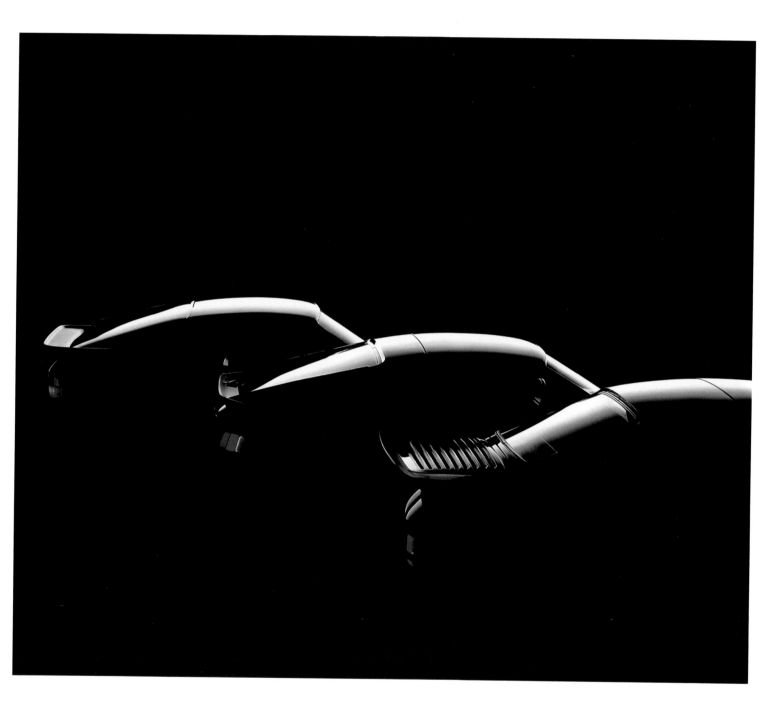

Dietmar Henneka
Photo design for Porsche

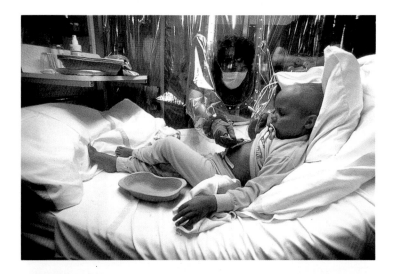

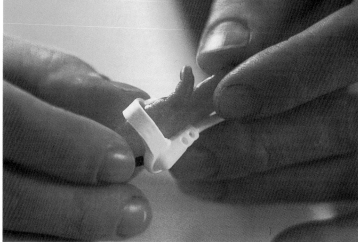

Wolfgang Kunz
The fight against leukemia

Thomas Stephan
Struggling for a handful of life

Timm Rautert
Columbia

Volker Hinz
Rich people of Palm Beach

Holger Eckstein
Nostalgic black-and-white

Matthew Rolston
Long neck

Matthew Rolston
Cindy Lauper

Matthew Rolston
George Michael

Matthew Rolston
Andie MacDowell

Matthew Rolston
Aly, "claw hand"

Matthew Rolston
Lysette Anthony, "reclining"

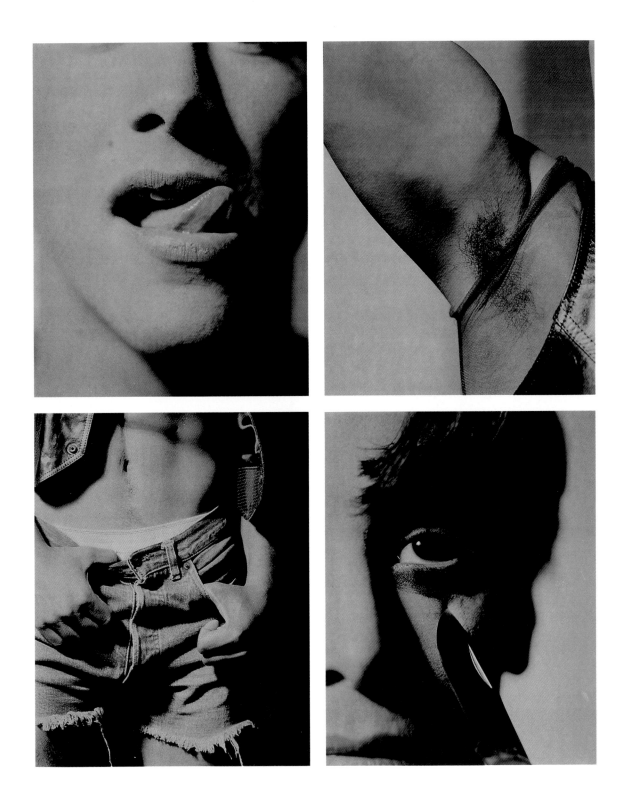

Matthew Rolston
*Keenu Reeves, "detail lips, detail arm,
detail waist, detail eye"*

Matthew Rolston
Ishbel, "as fire"

Matthew Rolston
Anitta, "clock fac

Matthew Rolston
Jodie Foster

Matthew Rolston
Lisa Bonet

Günther Raupp
Porsche 911 Carrera

Günther Raupp
Ferrari Testarossa

Nadav Kander
Children in yard

Nadav Kander
Hanging jacket

Nadav Kander
Pinnacles, Australia

Barossa Valley, Australia

Nadav Kander
Pink wall (Coca-Cola), Morocco

White rowing boat, Ireland

Ray Charles White
Adrian Leslie, lawyer

Ray Charles White
Dennis Hopper, actor

Ray Charles White
John Updike, writer
Katherine Helmond, actress
Billy Wilder, screenwriter
Tony Bennett, singer

Ray Charles White
Taylor Mead, actor

Gianfranco Gorgoni
Havana, Cuba

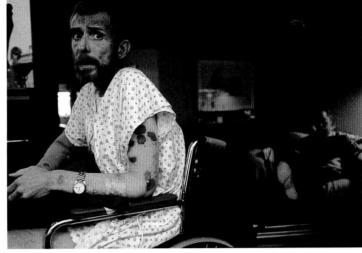

Frank Fournier
Family in home destroyed by guerilla shelling,
Baddawi, Lebanon

Alon Reininger
Sandinistas in Samoza's private gymnasium
after the revolution

Alon Reininger
Ken Meeks, patient with AIDS, San Francisco

Alon Reininger
Model family, China

Liu Heng Shing
Beijing, China

Gianfranco Gorgoni
Leo Castelli

Annie Leibovitz
Yoko Ono with John Lennon, taken the morning
of December 8, 1980
the day of Lennon's assassination

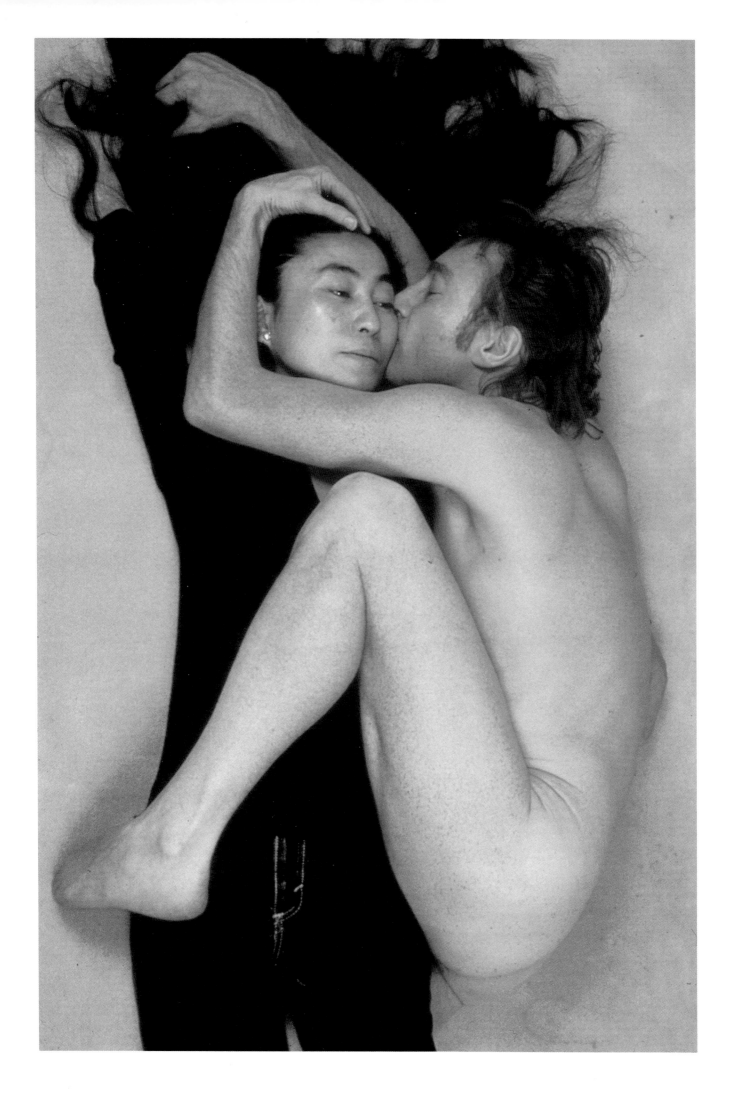

David Burnett
The US 82nd Airborne Division, Grenada

Dilip Mehta
Khabarovsk, USSR

David Burnett
Mary Decker, Final 3000 meter race of the
Los Angeles Olympics 1984

Dilip Mehta
Jain festival, Mysore, India

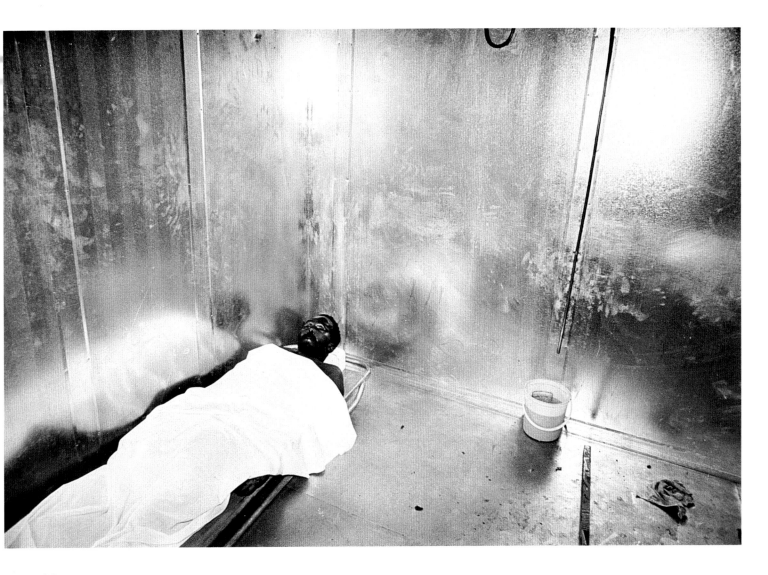

Matt Franjola
The body of Steven Biko in the morgue,
South Africa

Boris Smelov
Still life with a mirror

Vladimir Filonov
Reminiscences of Russian provinces

Victor Shurov
Boys

Lev Melihov
Erik Bulatov

Vladzimir P. Parfianok
Being a patron

Sergey Leontiev
Study in hard photography

Valery Potapov
Gates

Javier Vallhonrat (Photographer), Δ▷
Juan Gatti (Art Director)
Animal-vegetal

Javier Vallhonrat (Photographer),
Juan Gatti (Art Director)
Vogue jewelry

Javier Vallhonrat (Photographer),
Juan Gatti (Art Director)
Italian vogue

Javier Vallhonrat (Photographer),
Juan Gatti (Art Director)
Animal-vegetal

Javier Vallhonrat (Photographer),
Juan Gatti (Art Director)
The poetry of color
Untitled
Alphabet
Fall / Winter collection

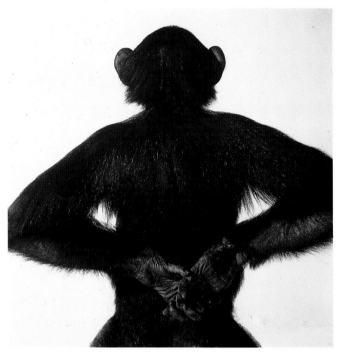

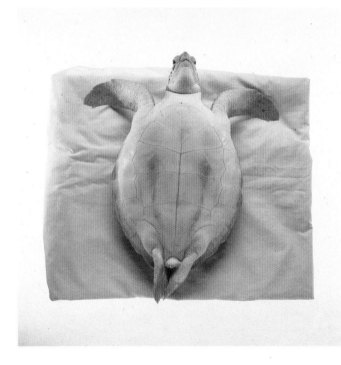

James Balog
Chimpanzee
Great grey owl
Atlantic green sea turtle
Morelet's crocodile

James Balog
Drill

James Balog
Florida panther

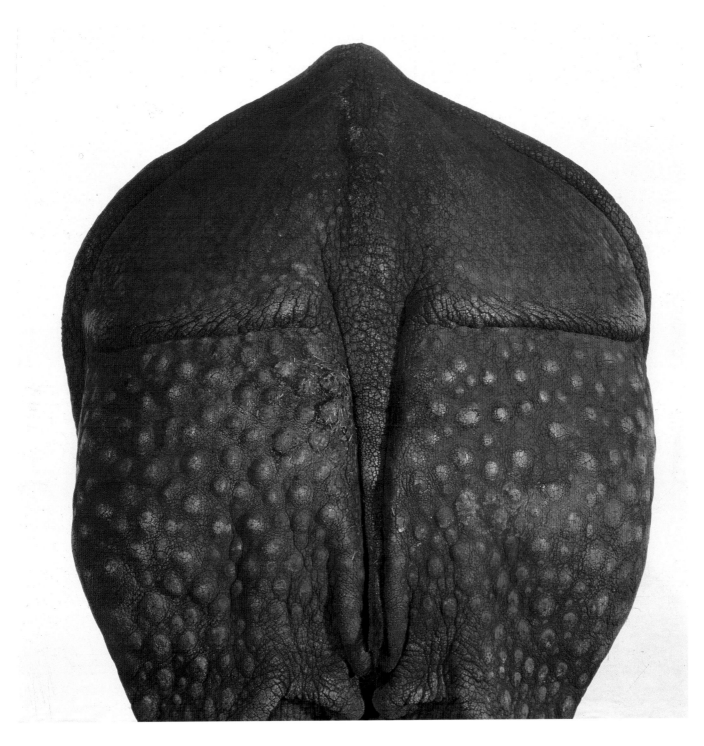

James Balog
Great Indian rhinocerous

Ann Rhoney
Spreckels
Books
Angel Island
Tapping for a new record

Ann Rhoney
Sally Robertson

Ann Rhoney
The high seats

Ann Rhoney
Middle aged orphan

Josef Astor
Peter and Dovanna

Josef Astor
If Thomas Jefferson were alive today

Josef Astor
The art of giving Christmas gifts

Josef Astor
The actor Julian Sands

John Isaac
Fantasia

Fabrizio Ferri
L'Oreal calendar

Teiji Saga
A snowdrift of swans

Brian Lanker
Eva Jessye

Laci Perényi
Stephanie Ortwig

Conny J. Winter
Fiat Uno

Conny J. Winter
Personal work

GRAPHIS

The International Magazine of Design and Communication

Die internationale Zeitschrift für Design und Kommunikation

Le magazine international du design et de la communication

Specifications:

112 Pages/Seiten

Published bi-monthly
Erscheint alle zwei Monate
Paraît tous les deux mois

Size: 9x12 inches
Format: 23x30 cm

Over 200 color plates
Über 200 Farbbilder
Plus de 200 pages en couleurs

Contents:

The name *Graphis* carries a special meaning that for 50 years has set it apart from all other design magazines. Every other month *Graphis* brings you in-depth profiles on creative leaders in graphic design, illustration, photography, advertising, product design, and architecture and interviews with CEO's of design-directed corporations.

From cover to cover, you'll find an unmatched selection of the best creative talents each field has to offer. Since powerful visions are best evoked through powerful voices, top writers reveal the motivations and inspiration of both past masters and today's luminaries from around the world.

The leading publication of visual communication, *Graphis* is admired internationally by readers who appreciate fine design and designers who appreciate a fine read. Lavishly printed,—*Graphis* will inspire and delight you as it seeks to enlarge the quality of design on every creative front.

For information and prices in US, Canada, Asia and Pacific see the attached subscription order form or call + 1 (212) 532 9387 or fax + 1 (212) 213 3229

GRAPHIS U.S., Inc.
141 Lexington Avenue
New York, NY 10016

For information and prices in Europe, Middle East and Africa see the attached order form or call + 41 (1) 383 8211 or fax + 41 (1) 383 1643

GRAPHIS Press Corp.
Dufourstrasse 107
CH-8008 Zürich, Switzerland

Inhalt:

Graphis ist seit 50 Jahren ein Begriff und hebt sich klar von anderen Design-Magazinen ab. Alle zwei Monate bringt Ihnen *Graphis* aufschlussreiche Berichte über die führenden kreativen Köpfe im Bereich des Graphik-Designs, der Illustration, der Photographie, der Werbung, der Produktgestaltung und der Architektur. Interviews mit Geschäftsführern designbewusster Unternehmen informieren über die Standpunkte der Auftraggeber.

Graphis bietet Ihnen von Ausgabe zu Ausgabe eine einmalige Auswahl der besten kreativen Leistungen in den verschiedenen Bereichen. Grosse Visionen – von grossen Stimmen kundgetan. Nur erstklassige Autoren schreiben über Motivation und Inspiration der Meister von gestern, heute und morgen – aus aller Welt. Führend im Bereich der visuellen Kommunikation, geniesst *Graphis*

international grosses Ansehen bei Lesern, die gutes Design fasziniert und bei Designern, die gute Texte schätzen. *Graphis* erscheint in allerbester Druckqualität. Das Ziel ist, in allen Bereichen des Designs hervorragende Qualität zu fördern. Lassen Sie sich von *Graphis* inspirieren und herausfordern, und messen Sie sich und Ihre Arbeit auf internationaler Ebene.

Preisinformation für Amerika, die Pazifikländer und Asien entnehmen Sie bitte der gegenüberliegenden Bestellkarte oder über:
Tel. + 1 212 532 9387 oder
Fax + 1 212 213 3229

GRAPHIS US Inc.
141 Lexington Avenue
New York, NY 10016

Preisinformation für West- und Osteuropa, den Mittleren Osten und Afrika entnehmen Sie bitte der gegenüberliegenden Bestellkarte oder über:
Tel. + 41 1 383 82 11 oder
Fax + 41 1 383 16 43

GRAPHIS Verlag
Dufourstrasse 107
CH-8008 Zürich, Schweiz

Sommaire:

Le nom de *Graphis* est une référence depuis 50 ans. D'emblée, ce magazine a su se distinguer des autres revues de design. Tous les deux mois, *Graphis* vous propose des reportages détaillés sur les meilleurs créatifs dans des domaines aussi variés que le design graphique, l'illustration, la photographie, la publicité, le design de produits et l'architecture. Vous y trouverez également des interviews de directeurs d'entreprises qui ont mis le design au rang de leurs priorités.

Dans chaque numéro, *Graphis* vous offre un choix unique des créations les plus remarquables réalisées dans ces divers secteurs d'activité. Des images exceptionnelles commentées par de grands noms. Vous découvrirez ainsi les motivations et les sources d'inspiration des plus grands créateurs contemporains du monde entier.

Leader dans le secteur de la communication visuelle, le magazine *Graphis* a acquis une réputation internationale auprès de lecteurs qui sont fascinés par l'esthétique du design et de professionnels qui apprécient de bons articles.

N'hésitez plus! Abonnez-vous dès maintenant à *Graphis*. Vous pourrez y puiser à loisir idées et suggestions. Il vous permettra aussi de vous situer par rapport à la concurrence internationale.

Vous trouverez le prix des abonnements pour l'Amérique, le Canada, l'Asie et la région du Pacifique sur la carte de commande de la page opposée. Pour plus d'information téléphonez au:
tél. + 1 212 532 9387
fax. + 1 212 213 3229

GRAPHIS US Inc.
141 Lexington Avenue
New York, NY 10016

Vous trouverez le prix des abonnements pour l'Europe (Est et Ouest), le Moyen-Orient et l'Afrique sur la carte de commande de la page opposée. Pour plus d'information téléphonez au:
tél. + 41 1 383 82 11
fax + 41 1 383 16 43

Editions GRAPHIS
Dufourstrasse 107
CH-8008 Zürich, Suisse

BUSINESS REPLY MAIL
FIRST CLASS PERMIT NO. 2207 NEW YORK NY

POSTAGE WILL BE PAID BY ADDRESSEE

GRAPHIS US INC
141 LEXINGTON AVENUE
NEW YORK NY 10157-1003

GRAPHIS PRESS CORP.
DUFOURSTRASSE 107
CH-8008 ZURICH
SWITZERLAND